74 Great-Tasting Chili Recipes
for the Chili Lover

Kathryn Marie Carriere

Note for Librarians: A cataloguing record for this book is available from Library and Archives Canada at www.collectionscanada.ca/amicus/index-e.html
ISBN 1-4251-1556-X

PUBLISHING™
Offices in Canada, USA, Ireland and UK

Book sales for North America and international:
Trafford Publishing, 6E–2333 Government St.,
Victoria, BC V8T 4P4 CANADA
phone 250 383 6864 (toll-free 1 888 232 4444)
fax 250 383 6804; email to orders@trafford.com
Book sales in Europe:
Trafford Publishing (UK) Limited, 9 Park End Street, 2nd Floor
Oxford, UK OX1 1HH UNITED KINGDOM
phone +44 (0)1865 722 113 (local rate 0845 230 9601)
facsimile +44 (0)1865 722 868; info.uk@trafford.com
Order online at:
trafford.com/06-3302

10 9 8 7 6 5 4 3 2 1

Dedication

To the students, faculty and staff of Our Lady of Mt. Carmel Catholic School. Always believe in yourself and you will be successful. Remember to always have God first and foremost in your life.

Kathleen Wagner who always believed when no one else did.

Abigail Doheny who is a "stress buddy."

Foreword

74 Great-Tasting Chili Recipes for the Chili Lover is composed of recipes that are considered to be in the public domain. The author collected these recipes from public domain sources, primarily Internet recipe archives. Care was taken to remove any recipes that included copyright text. Some recipes were missing their attributions, so if you see anything that is copyrighted, please let us know so we can remove it. The author and the publisher cannot be held liable for the inclusion of any copyrighted material in this collection. All restaurant and product names are trademarks of their respective owners.

Table of Contents

Alaska Pipeline Chili

5 pounds moose meat
1 pound bacon, diced Garlic, to taste
2 to 4 onions, chopped
2 to 6 tablespoons chili powder, to taste
2 tablespoons cumin, or to taste
2 (16 ounce) cans tomatoes, undrained

Cook bacon until it there is a large amount of bacon grease in the pan. Add moose meat, onions and garlic, and cook until meat is browned, stirring often. Add chili powder, cumin and tomatoes and simmer until meat is tender. If more liquid is needed, add a little water or beer.

Alamo Chili

2 lb Stew meat
1 md Onion
1 cn Tomato sauce
2   Cloves garlic
2 tb of chili powder
2   Jalapeno chilis
2 c Pinto beans
Salt and pepper to taste

Trim the fat from the stew meat, cut into bite sized chunks and brown it. Chop the onion and the jalapeno chili. Smash the garlic. Throw every thing but the beans into a pot, add water and simmer until meat is tender.

Put the beans into a pot with water and bring to a boil, turn the heat down and simmer till the beans are done.

Eat the chili and stomp the hell out of the beans.

Don't confuse this with "Rebel Chile" which also has the beans stomped out of it.

I brought this recipe back from Mexico and it was said to be the one that Mexico used when they taught Texans how to make chili at the Alamo. I understand that to this day Texans do not put beans in chili.

TL: If it hasn't got a bean it must be Texas.

All-Bean Chili

1 onion, chopped
1 green bell pepper, diced
2 cloves garlic
1 tablespoon olive oil
1/2 teaspoon ground cumin
1 tablespoon chili powder
1/2 teaspoon dried oregano
2 cups canned pinto or kidney beans,
rinsed and drained
1/2 cup water
1/4 teaspoon salt
Fresh cilantro, chopped

In a nonstick skillet, sauté onion, green pepper and garlic in olive oil over medium heat until soft, about 5 minutes. Add cumin, chili powder and oregano; cook 1 minute. Add beans, water and salt, and cook another 15 minutes.

Serve garnished with cilantro.

All-Beef Texas Chili

1/3 cup(approximately) corn oil
6 pounds   beef chuck -- in 1/2-inch cubes
1 cup   minced onion
1/3 cup   minced garlic
3 cups   (approximately) beef broth
3 cups   flat beer
1 ½ cups   water
1/4 cup   high-quality chili powder,
 or more -- to taste
6 pounds   tomatoes (three 2 lb. cans) -- drained
and chopped
1/3 cup   tomato paste
1 1/2 tablespoons   minced fresh oregano
3   tablespoons   cumin seed
Salt -- to taste
Cayenne pepper -- to taste
Masa harina or cornmeal -- if needed

1. In a large heavy skillet over moderately high heat,
warm 3 tablespoons of the oil. Brown beef in batches,
adding more oil as necessary and transferring meat with
a slotted spoon to a large stockpot when well browned.
Do not crowd skillet.

2. Reduce heat to moderately low. Add onion and garlic
and sauté until softened (about 10 minutes). Add to
stockpot along with broth, beer, the water, chili powder,
tomato, tomato paste, and oregano.

3. In a small skillet over low heat, toast cumin seed until
fragrant; do not allow to burn. Grind in an electric
minichopper or with a mortar and pestle. Add to stockpot.

4. Over high heat bring mixture to a simmer. Add salt, cayenne, and more chili powder to taste. Reduce heat to maintain a simmer and cook, partially covered, until beef is tender (about 1-1/2 hours). Check occasionally and add more broth if mixture seems dry. If chili is too thin when meat is tender, stir in up to 2 tablespoons masa harina. Cook an additional 5 minutes to thicken. Serve chili hot.

NOTES : No Texan worth his or her ten-gallon hat would put beans in chili. This one's all beef, calling on beer and freshly ground cumin to give it distinction. Masa harina, the finely ground corn used for corn tortillas, is often used to thicken soups or chili. It is available in Latin markets and some supermarkets.

Amarillo Chili

4 slices bacon, cut into 1/2-inch pieces
2 onions
1 garlic clove
1/2 pound pork shoulder, coarsely ground
1 pound beef round, cut into 1/2-inch strips
1/2 pound beef chuck, coarsely ground
2 to 4 jalapeño chiles, diced
1 tablespoon ground hot red chile
2 tablespoons ground mild red chile
1 teaspoon dried Mexican oregano
1 1/2 teaspoons cumin (comino)
1 1/2 teaspoons salt
12 ounces tomato paste
3 cups water
1 (16 ounce) can pinto beans

Fry bacon in a large, deep heavy pot over medium heat. When the bacon has rendered most of its fat, remove the pieces with a slotted spoon, drain on paper toweling and reserve. Add the onions and garlic to the bacon fat and cook until the onions are translucent.

Add the pork and beef to the pot. Break up any lumps with a fork and cook over medium-high heat, stirring occasionally, until the meat is evenly browned.

Stir in the remaining ingredients except the beans and the bacon. Bring to a boil, then lower the heat and simmer, uncovered, for 2 hours, stirring occasionally.

Taste and adjust seasonings. Stir in the beans and the bacon, and simmer for 1/2 hour longer.

Arizona Chicken Chili

Makes 4 servings. Serve with cornbread.

1 tablespoon oil
1 pound boneless, skinless chicken
breasts, cut into 1-inch chunks
2 tablespoons Santa Fe style spice blend
(chili, cumin and garlic)
1 (14 1/2 ounce) can diced tomatoes
1 (11 ounce) can whole kernel corn
1 (14 1/2 ounce) can kidney beans

Heat oil in large skillet. Add chicken cubes.
Cook for 5 to 6 minutes.

Stir in remaining ingredients; simmer, uncovered, 10 minutes.

Top with shredded Cheddar cheese, if desired.

Australian Dinkum Chili

Yield: 8 servings

1/2 pound bacon
2 tablespoons vegetable oil
2 medium onions, coarsely chopped
1 celery stalk, coarsely chopped
1 bell peppers, chopped
1 (2 pound) top beef sirloin, 1-inch cubes
1 pound beef, hamburger grind
1 pound pork, hamburger grind
4 tablespoons ground hot red chile
3 tablespoons ground mild red chile
2 garlic cloves, finely chopped
1 tablespoon dried Mexican oregano
1 teaspoon ground cumin
2 (12 ounce) cans Australian beer
1 (14 1/2 ounce) can whole tomatoes
3 teaspoons brown sugar
1 Boomerang (optional, but authentic)

Fry the bacon in a skillet over medium heat. Drain the strips on paper toweling and cut into 1/2-inch dice and reserve.

Heat the oil in a large heavy pot over medium heat. Add the onions, celery, and green pepper and cook until the onions are translucent.

Combine all the beef and pork with the ground chile, garlic, oregano, and cumin. Add this meat-and-spice mixture to the pot.

Break up any lumps with a fork and cook, stirring occasionally, until the meat is evenly browned.

Add the beer, tomatoes and reserved bacon to the pot. Bring to a boil, then lower the heat and simmer, uncovered, for 1 1/2 hours. Wave a boomerang over the pot 14 times each hour from this point on. (This is definitely optional adding no noticeable flavor, just a touch of authenticity and humor.) Stir for 3 minutes. Taste, adjust seasonings, and add more beer if desired. Simmer for 2 1/2 hours longer.

Add the brown sugar and simmer for 15 minutes longer, vigorously waving the boomerang over the pot.

Authentic Texas Border Chili

Yield: 12 servings

3 medium tomatoes
1 large Bermuda onion, finely chopped
1/4 teaspoon dried Mexican oregano
2 teaspoons paprika
5 large garlic cloves, finely chopped
1 (4 pound) beef shank, coarsely ground
1 tablespoon lard, butter or bacon drippings
4 scallions, chopped
5 green bell peppers, chopped
5 fresh Serrano chiles, chopped
1 pound chorizo sausage or hot non-Italian sausage
4 medium garlic cloves, finely chopped
2 teaspoons salt
4 tablespoons ground hot red chile
4 tablespoons ground mild red chile
3 tablespoons cumin seeds
Beer
Water

Puree the first four ingredients plus one clove of the garlic in a blender or food processor (using the steel blade). Scrape the mixture into a large heavy pot and add the beef.

Melt the lard, butter, or bacon drippings in a heavy skillet over medium heat. Add the scallions, bell peppers, serrano chiles, sausage, and the remaining garlic, and cook until the onions are translucent and the sausage is browned.

Place the cumin seeds in a 300 degree F oven for a few minutes until lightly browned. Remove seeds from the oven and crush them with a mallet. Stir the vegetables into the beef and tomato mixture. Add the salt ground chile, cumin, and enough water or beer to cover. Bring to a boil over medium-high heat, then lower the heat and simmer, uncovered for 4 to 6 hours. Taste and adjust seasonings.

Black Bean Chili

1 pound black beans or 4 cans black beans, drained
2 cups tomatoes, puréed
2 to 3 cups vegetable broth, water or chicken broth
1 onion, chopped
1 teaspoon garlic, minced
2 teaspoons chili powder
1 teaspoon dried leaf oregano
1/2 teaspoon cumin
1/2 teaspoon salt, or to taste
Freshly-ground pepper, to taste

If using dried beans, clean and soak beans overnight, then drain. Cover with fresh water and cook until tender, about 2 hours. Drain.

In large pot, combine drained beans with all other ingredients except salt and pepper. Cover and simmer for 1 hour. Season to taste. Serve with garnishes such as salsa, chopped onions and grated cheese, if desired.

Bourbon Chili

4 pounds lean ground beef
1 cup Bourbon
3/4 cup chili powder
1 teaspoon oregano
1 tablespoon diced onion
3/4 teaspoon salt
1 (16 ounce) can kidney beans
2 ounces semisweet chocolate
1 (8 ounce) can tomato sauce
6 (8 ounce) cans water
1 teaspoon cumin
2 teaspoons paprika
2 teaspoons garlic powder
4 small cans chopped green chiles
1 (14 ounce) can whole corn

Brown ground beef and drain off fat. Add ingredients one at a time in order listed. Simmer 1 to 1 1/2 hours.

Makes about 1 1/2 gallons of chili.

Bowl of Red Chili

12 dried ancho chiles
3 pounds lean beef chuck, cut into thumb-
size pieces
2 ounces beef suet
1 tablespoon ground cumin
1 tablespoon dried oregano
1 tablespoon cayenne
1 tablespoon Tabasco sauce
2 or more garlic cloves, chopped
1 tablespoon salt
2 tablespoons Masa Harina (optional)

Break off stems of chiles and remove
seeds. Place chiles in a small saucepan,
cover them with water. Simmer the chiles
for 30 minutes. Purée chiles in a blender
with a bit of their cooking liquid to make a
smooth, thin paste. Use as little liquid as
possible, unless you want the chili to be
soupy. Pour the chile purée into a Dutch
oven.

In a heavy skillet, sear the meat in two
batches with the beef suet until the meat is
gray. Transfer each batch to the chile purée, then pour in enough of the chile cooking liquid to cover the meat by about 2
inches. Bring the chili to a boil, and then
reduce the heat to a simmer. Cook the chili
30 minutes. Remove the chili from the
heat, and stir in the remaining ingredients.
Return the chili to the heat, and resume

simmering for 45 minutes, keeping the lid on except to stir occasionally (too much stirring will tear up the meat). Add more chile cooking liquid only if you think the mixture will burn otherwise.

After 45 minutes, add the Masa Harina if you wish. It will add a subtle, tamale-like taste to the chile and will thicken or "tighten" the chili. Cover the chili again, and simmer it for another 30 minutes, until the meat is done. Adjust seasonings during this time. Take the chile off the heat and re-frigerate it overnight.

Skim as much fat as you wish from the chili before re-heating it. Serve it hot.

Buzzard's Breath Chili

8 pounds beef (US Choice boneless chuck)
3 (8 ounce) cans tomato sauce
2 large onions, chopped
5 cloves garlic, crushed and chopped
2 jalapeno peppers
Chili powder (about twice the label amount)
2 teaspoons ground cumin
1/4 to 1/2 teaspoon oregano
Salt to taste
1 to 2 teaspoons paprika
Cayenne pepper to taste
Masa Harina (as needed)
1 quart beef stock

Take meat and chop into 3/8-inch cubes, removing all gristle and visible fat. Brown in an iron skillet, about 2 pounds at a time. Place in a large cast-iron chili pot, adding tomato sauce and equal amounts of water. Add chopped onion, garlic, jalapeno peppers (wrapped in cheesecloth) and chili powder. Simmer for 20 minutes, then add the cumin, oregano, salt and cayenne pepper to taste. As moisture is required, add homemade beef stock until amount is used, then add water if needed. Simmer, covered, until meat is tender (about 2 hours), stirring occasionally. Then add the Masa Harina to thicken if needed. Add paprika for color. Cook 10 additional minutes; correct the seasoning. Discard the jalapenos and serve.

A small additional amount of cumin enhances aroma when added in the last ten minutes.

Cajun Chili

1 1/2 pounds ground beef
1 pound ground hot sausage
2 (8 ounce) cans tomato sauce
1 (10 ounce) can diced tomatoes and
green chiles
1 (32 ounce) can prepared chili (Gebhardt)
1 (16 ounce) can ranch-style chili beans
(optional)
1 large onion, chopped
1 large green bell pepper, chopped
1 to 2 tablespoons minced garlic
Cajun seasoning

Brown ground beef and ground sausage; drain grease. Add seasonings and vegetables. Simmer until vegetables are tender. Add all other ingredients and simmer about 30 minutes or to desired consistency.

Serve with shredded cheese and sour cream.

Cajun Pork Chili

2 pounds ground pork
2 large onions, chopped
4 cloves garlic, minced
1 sweet red bell pepper, chopped
1 sweet green bell pepper, chopped
3 stalks celery, chopped
1 (28 ounce) can tomatoes
1 (28 ounce) can kidney beans, drained
1/4 teaspoon hot pepper flakes
1 teaspoon dried oregano
1/4 teaspoon cayenne pepper
Dash of hot pepper sauce
Salt and pepper

If you prefer a more traditional chili flavor, use cumin instead of oregano, and add chili powder to taste.

In a heavy saucepan, cook the pork over medium heat, stirring to break up the meat, for about 5 minutes or until browned. Pour off the fat.

Add onions, and cook until tender. Add garlic, red and green peppers and celery. Cook, stirring occasionally, for 5 minutes or until vegetables are softened.

Add tomatoes, breaking them up with the back of a spoon. Stir in kidney beans, hot pepper flakes, oregano, cayenne pepper, hot pepper sauce and salt and pepper to taste. Bring to a boil; reduce heat and simmer for 20 minutes.

Capital Punishment Chili

Servings: 4

    1 tb Oregano
    2 tb Paprika
    2 tb MSG (monosodium glutamate)
    9 tb Chili powder, light
    4 tb Cumin
    4 tb Beef bouillon
        (instant, crushed)
   24 oz Old Milwaukee beer
    2 c Water
    4 lb Extra lean chuck,
        Chili grind
    2 lb Extra lean pork,
        Chili grind
    1 lb Extra lean chuck,
        Cut into 1/4" cubes
    2   Large onions, finely chopped
   10   Cloves garlic,
        Finely chopped
  1/2 c Wesson oil or kidney suet
    1 ts Mole (powdered),
        Also called mole poblano
    1 tb Sugar
    1 ts Coriander seed (from Chinese
        Parsley, cilantro)
    1 ts Louisiana Red Hot Sauce
        (Durkee's)
    8 oz Tomato sauce
    1 tb Masa Harina flour
        Salt to taste

In a large pot, add paprika, oregano, MSG, chili powder, cumin, beef bouillon, beer and 2 cups water. Let simmer.

In a separate skillet, brown meat in 1 lb. or 1 1/2 lb. batches with Wesson oil or suet. Drain and add to simmering spices. Continue   until all meat is done.

Sauté chopped onion and garlic in 1 T. oil or suet. Add to spices   and meat mixture. Add water as needed. Simmer 2 hours. Add mole, sugar, coriander seed, hot sauce and tomato sauce. Simmer 45 min.

Dissolve masa harina flour in warm water to form a paste. Add to   chili. Add salt to taste. Simmer for 30 minutes. Add additional   Louisiana Hot Sauce for hotter taste.

Makes 1 pot.

Cheesy Chili

1 (15 ounce) can chili
1 (14 ounce) can diced tomatoes
1 cup Minute Rice
I cup water
1 1/2 cups shredded cheese of your choice
Salt and pepper to taste

Bring chili, water and tomatoes to boil in a large frying pan. Once it is boiling, add the Minute Rice and simmer for one to two minutes. Remove from heat and sprinkle cheese over the top and serve. Also tastes great with sour cream and buttered bread.

Cheesy Potato and Bacon Chili

2 tablespoons vegetable oil
1 pound potatoes, peeled, cut into 1/2-inch pieces
1 onion, chopped
2 cloves garlic, minced
1 (28 ounce) can whole peeled tomatoes, broken up, undrained
1 (8 ounce) can tomato sauce
1/2 cup water
1 tablespoon chili powder
1 small green bell pepper, diced
1/4 cup chopped parsley
1/4 cup prepared horseradish
6 strips crisp cooked bacon, crumbled
1/2 cup shredded Cheddar cheese

Heat the oil in a 2-quart pot. Add the potatoes, onion, and garlic. Sauté 5 minutes.

Add the next 4 ingredients. Bring to a boil, reduce the heat, cover, and simmer 10 minutes. Uncover and stir in remaining ingredients except cheese. Cook 5 minutes more or until desired consistency. Garnish each serving with cheese.

Serves 4.

Chicken Chili

1/2 pound boneless skinless chicken
breasts, cut into 1-inch pieces
3/4 cup chopped onion
1/2 cup chopped green bell pepper
2 garlic cloves, minced
1 (15 ounce) can garbanzo, white or red
kidney beans, drained
1 (14 1/2 ounce) can diced tomatoes
1 cup chicken broth
1/2 cup tomato catsup
1 tablespoon chili powder
1/8 teaspoon crushed red pepper
Sour cream (optional)
Shredded cheese (optional)
Tortilla chips (optional)

In medium skillet coated with nonstick
cooking spray, cook chicken, onion, pepper
and garlic over medium-high heat until
chicken is no longer pink, stirring constantly. Add beans, tomatoes, broth, catsup, chili powder and red pepper. Cover;
simmer 10 minutes.

Serve with sour cream, shredded cheese
and tortilla chips if desired.

Chicken Chili II

8 chicken breasts, boned and skinned
2 tablespoons vegetable oil
1 medium onion, chopped
1 medium bell pepper, chopped
2 cloves garlic, minced
4 (16 ounce) cans chicken broth
2 (16 ounce) cans great northern beans
2 teaspoons chili powder
2 teaspoons ground cumin
1 teaspoon salt
1 large can diced tomatoes
1 1/2 cups dry macaroni
Avocados, chopped (garnish)
Chopped onion (garnish)
Shredded cheese (garnish)

Cut chicken in bite-size pieces.

Heat oil in Dutch oven. Add chicken, onion, bell pepper and garlic. Cook until the chicken is lightly browned.

Add broth and remaining ingredients. Cover and simmer until macaroni is done. Serve topped with chopped avocados, chopped onion or shredded cheese. Season to your taste.

Chili Verde

1 pound pork or beef
Oil or lard
4 green chiles, toasted, peeled and
chopped
2 cloves garlic, crushed
1 medium onion, chopped
1 medium tomato, chopped
1 cup boiling water
Salt
Pepper

Cut pork into small cubes. Sauté in oil until well browned. Drain off all but 1 tablespoon fat. Add chopped chiles, garlic, onion, tomato and water and season to taste with salt and pepper. If desired, you may also add 1 potato, peeled and diced, at this time. Cover tightly and simmer for 1 hour.

Chili with Corn Dumplings

1 1/2 pounds ground beef
3/4 cup chopped onion
1 (15 to 17 ounce) can whole kernel corn,
undrained
1 (16 ounce) can stewed tomatoes,
undrained
1 (16 ounce) can tomato sauce
2 tablespoons chili powder
1 teaspoon minced garlic
1 teaspoon red pepper sauce
1 1/3 cups Bisquick Original baking mix
2/3 cup cornmeal
2/3 cup milk
3 tablespoons chopped fresh cilantro

Cook beef and onion in Dutch oven over medium heat, stirring occasionally, until beef is brown; drain.

Reserve 1/2 cup of the corn. Stir in remaining corn with liquid, tomatoes, tomato sauce, chili powder, garlic salt and red pepper sauce into beef mixture. Heat to boiling; reduce heat. Cover and simmer 15 minutes.

Mix baking mix and cornmeal. Stir in milk, cilantro and reserved 1/2 cup corn just until moist. Drop dough by rounded tablespoonfuls onto simmering chili. Cook uncovered over low heat 15 minutes. Cover and cook 15 to 18 minutes or until dumplings are dry.

Cincinnati Chili

"Two way" - Sauce comes on a pile of spaghetti
"Three-way" - Spaghetti topped with chili and grated cheddar cheese
"Four-way" - Adds chopped onions
"Five-way" - Adds beans

1 1/2 pounds lean ground sirloin
1 small onion, chopped
1 (20 ounce) can tomato sauce
1 (14 ounce) can whole tomatoes
1/2 teaspoon cinnamon
1/2 teaspoon allspice
1 teaspoon salt
1/2 teaspoon pepper
1 1/2 tablespoons chili powder
1 tablespoon vinegar
1 clove garlic
3 bay leaves

Brown meat and chopped onions. Drain grease. Place meat and onions in a large pan or crockpot with all other ingredients. Cook slowly for 4 to 5 hours, covered.

Remove bay leaves and garlic before serving. Serve any way you like.

Cocoa Chili

"Two way" - Sauce comes on a pile of spa-
ghetti
"Three-way" - Spaghetti topped with chili
and grated cheddar cheese
"Four-way" - Adds chopped onions
"Five-way" - Adds beans

1 1/2 pounds lean ground sirloin
1 small onion, chopped
1 (20 ounce) can tomato sauce
1 (14 ounce) can whole tomatoes
1/2 teaspoon cinnamon
1/2 teaspoon allspice
1 teaspoon salt
1/2 teaspoon pepper
1 1/2 tablespoons chili powder
1 tablespoon vinegar
1 clove garlic
3 bay leaves

Brown meat and chopped onions. Drain
grease. Place meat and onions in a large
pan or crockpot with all other ingredients.
Cook slowly for 4 to 5 hours, covered.

Remove bay leaves and garlic before serving. Serve any way you like.

Colorado River Chili

3 teaspoons lemon juice
2 pounds ground turkey
1 garlic clove, chopped
1 small onion, chopped
1 cup green bell pepper, chopped
2 (15 ounce) cans stewed tomatoes
1 (6 ounce) can tomato paste
1 cup red kidney beans, cooked
1 (15 ounce) can corn
2 teaspoons ground pepper
1 teaspoon chili pepper
1/4 cup salsa

Put lemon juice in a large nonstick frying pan, then add the turkey, garlic, onion and green pepper. Cook until turkey is browned. Add and combine the remaining ingredients and simmer for 30 minutes.

Serves 4.

Coors Spicy Chili

2 strips bacon
2 pounds beef chuck, diced
2 (12 ounce) cans Coors Beer
2 tablespoons chili powder
1 tablespoon dried oregano, crushed
1 tablespoon ground cumin
1/2 teaspoon cayenne pepper
2 teaspoons Worcestershire sauce
1 tablespoon cornmeal or Masa Harina
Cooked pinto beans

Cook bacon until crisp; drain, reserving drippings in pan. Crumble bacon; set aside.

In drippings, brown meat. Add next 6 ingredients and 1 teaspoon salt. Bring to boiling; reduce heat. Simmer, covered, 45 minutes.

Combine cornmeal and 1/4 cup water. Stir into hot mixture; add crumbled bacon. Return to boiling. Reduce heat; simmer, covered, 15 minutes. Serve with beans.

Serves 8.

Corn Bread Cups

A different and elegant way to serve chili!

Yields 8 servings.

6 tablespoons butter, at room temperature
3 ounces cream cheese, at room temperature
1 tablespoon red bell pepper, chopped
1 tablespoon scallion, chopped
1 cup all-purpose flour
1/2 cup yellow cornmeal
1 pinch salt

Preheat oven to 350 degrees F.

Cream butter and cream cheese together in mixer. Add red pepper and scallions.

Mix flour, cornmeal and salt together and add it, a little at a time, to the butter mixture, stirring constantly until well blended. Remove from mixer bowl and knead with your hands. Make 2-inch balls of the dough and press into medium size muffin tins, being sure to press the dough evenly and completely up the side of the cup. Bake for 20 minutes or until golden brown.

Creamy White Chili

1 pound boneless skinless chicken breasts,
   cut into 1/2-inch pieces
1 medium onion, chopped
1 1/2 teaspoons garlic powder
1 tablespoon vegetable oil
2 (15 1/2 ounce) cans great northern
beans, rinsed and drained
1 (14 1/2 ounce) can chicken broth
2 (4 ounce) cans chopped green chiles
1 teaspoon salt
1 teaspoon ground cumin
1 teaspoon dried oregano
1/2 teaspoon pepper
1/4 teaspoon cayenne pepper
1 cup sour cream
1/2 cup whipping cream

In large skillet, sauté chicken, onions and
garlic power in oil until chicken is no longer
pink. Add beans, broth, chiles and seasonings. Bring to a boil. Reduce heat; simmer,
uncovered, for 30 minutes. Remove from
heat; stir in sour cream and cream. Serve
immediately.

Dallas Chili

Yield: 12 servings

6 pounds beef brisket, coarse grind
4 tablespoons ground hot red chile
1 tablespoon ground mild red chile
1/2 tablespoon chile Caribe
1 teaspoon cayenne pepper
2 tablespoons dried Mexican oregano
8 garlic cloves, crushed
4 bay leaves
1 teaspoon gumbo file (ground sassafras)
3 tablespoons ground cumin
3 tablespoons Woodruff or 2 ounces unsweetened chocolate
1 teaspoon paprika
1 tablespoon salt
1/3 cup bacon drippings
2 tablespoons lemon juice
2 tablespoons lime juice
1 tablespoon Dijon mustard
2 tablespoons Masa Harina
4 (12 ounce) cans beer
1 tablespoon Worcestershire sauce
1 tablespoon granulated sugar
1 tablespoon chicken fat (optional)
Hot pepper sauce (optional)

Combine the beef with the ground chile,
caribe, cayenne pepper, oregano, garlic,
bay leaves, gumbo file, cumin, woodruff (if
used), paprika and salt.

Heat the bacon drippings in a large heavy pot over medium heat. Add the meat and spice mixture to the pot. Break up any lumps with a fork and cook, stirring occasionally, until the meat is evenly browned.

Stir in the remaining ingredients (including the chocolate, if used) and the optional chicken fat and hot pepper sauce. Bring to a boil, then lower the heat and simmer, uncovered, for 2 hours. Taste and adjust seasonings.

Simmer, uncovered, for 10 hours longer, adding more beer or water and stirring as needed. Skim off fat before serving.

Dead Man's Chili

Yield: 6 to 8 servings.

1/4 cup chopped green and/or red bell pepper
1 pound lean beef, coarsely chopped
3 cups stewed chopped tomatoes
1 1/2 cups tomato paste
4 tablespoons chili powder
6 whole jalapeno peppers
1 1/2 teaspoons cayenne flakes
1 1/2 teaspoons salt
4 tablespoon freshly ground cumin, divided
1 tablespoon blackstrap molasses
3 medium onions, coarsely chopped
12 ounces beer (not lite)
1 teaspoon Angostura Bitters
4 ounces sour mash whiskey
3 bay leaves
1/4 cup yellow Masa Harina
2 ounces tequila
2 1/2 pounds coarsely ground beef chuck
6 cloves garlic, minced

Cook meat, 1 clove of garlic and 1 onion together. Mix all other ingredients except 1 tablespoon of cumin together and pour over meat in a large pot. Bring slowly to a boil and stir continuously until boiling. Cook at a boil for 10 minutes and then lower heat to medium-low for 15 minutes, stirring several times.

Lower heat again to simmer and cook for 1 1/2 to 2 hours, stirring frequently. Add remaining cumin after cooking for 1 hour. You may make this hotter by slashing the sides of the jalapeno peppers and by adding more of them.

Serve over rice with hot cornbread. Great when served over scrambled eggs as well.

Easy Hearty Chili

1 pound ground beef
1 (14.5 ounce) can Ro-Tel
1 (15 ounce) can kidney or pinto beans,
rinsed and drained
1 (1.25 ounce) envelope chili seasoning

Brown meat; drain. Add remaining ingredients. Simmer 15 minutes.

Yield: 4 to 6 servings.

Easy Pork Chili

1 1/2 pounds boneless pork loin, cut into 1-inch cubes
1 tablespoon vegetable oil
1/2 cup chopped onion
1 clove garlic, minced
1 tablespoon all-purpose flour
1 quart V-8 tomato juice
1 (14 1/2 ounce) can diced tomatoes
1 (16 ounce) can chili beans, drained
2 tablespoons chili powder
1 teaspoon salt
1/2 teaspoon black pepper

Heat oil in 4-quart Dutch oven over medium heat. Add pork, onion and garlic. Cook, stirring occasionally, until pork is browned. Thoroughly stir in flour. Add remaining ingredients and simmer, uncovered, one hour.

Serve, sprinkled with Cheddar cheese, if desired. Garnish each serving with a sprig of cilantro.

Five Can Chili

Servings: 6

1 (15 ounce) can chili with beans
1 (15 ounce) can mixed vegetables,
drained
1 (11 ounce) can corn, drained
1 (10 3/4 ounce) can condensed tomato
soup
1 (10 ounce) can tomatoes with green
chiles, diced

In a saucepan, combine all ingredients;
heat through.

Serves 6.

Frijole Mole Chili

Yield: 6 servings

2 cups coarsely chopped onions
2 cloves garlic, minced
2 tablespoons vegetable oil
1 (15 ounce) can dark red kidney beans,
rinsed and drained
1 (15 ounce) can black beans, rinsed and
drained
1 (15 ounce) can pinto beans, rinsed and
drained
1 (28 ounce) can whole tomatoes,
undrained, coarsely chopped
1 large green bell pepper, cut into 1/2-inch
pieces
1 cup picante sauce
2 tablespoons unsweetened cocoa
2 teaspoons ground cumin
1 teaspoon oregano leaves, crushed
1/2 teaspoon salt
1/8 teaspoon ground nutmeg
1/8 teaspoon ground allspice
Dash of ground cloves (optional)

Optional Toppings
Sour cream
Chopped cilantro
Shredded Monterey jack cheese

Cook onion and garlic in oil in large saucepan or Dutch oven until onion is tender but
not brown.

Add remaining ingredients except optional toppings; bring to a boil.

Reduce heat; cover and simmer 10 minutes. Uncover; continue to simmer 10 minutes, stirring occasionally.

Ladle into bowls; garnish as desired and serve with additional picante sauce.

Makes 6 servings - about 8 cups.

Georgia Chain Gang Chili

1 cup dry Burgundy
1/2 teaspoon dried thyme
2 bay leaves
4 medium garlic cloves, finely chopped
1/2 teaspoon freshly ground black pepper
6 pounds beef, coarsely ground
2 large chicken breasts
Water
2 teaspoons salt
2 tablespoons vegetable oil
2 onions
3 pork chops, coarse grind
10 tablespoons ground mild red chile
1 teaspoon cayenne pepper
1 teaspoon dried Mexican oregano
1/2 teaspoon cumin
Rosemary
1 1/2 cup Italian-style tomatoes
1 (16 ounce) can tomato sauce
1 (8 ounce) can hot Mexican tomato sauce
1 can whole mid green chiles
1 can pickled jalapeno peppers
2 tablespoons liquid hot pepper sauce
1 tablespoon butter
3 fresh whole green chiles
1/2 cup mushrooms
1/2 cup Sauterne
12 ounces beer

In a large non-aluminum (preferably glass
or glazed cast iron) bowl make a marinade
by combining the burgundy, thyme, bay

leaves, garlic, and black pepper. Place all the beef in the bowl and mix lightly to coat the meat well. Cover and refrigerate overnight. (If time is short marinate for 2 hours at room temperature.)

Place the chicken breasts in a saucepan with enough water to cover. Add 1 teaspoon salt and simmer over low heat for 1/2 hour. Remove the chicken reserving the liquid. Chop the chicken breasts fine and reserve.

Heat the oil in a large heavy pot. Add the onions and cook until they are translucent.

Meanwhile, drain the beef, straining and reserving the marinade. Mix the beef and pork together, then combine the meats with the ground chile, cayenne pepper, oregano, cumin, rosemary, and the rest of the salt. Add this meat and spice mixture to the pot with the onions. Break up any lumps with a fork and cook, stirring occasionally, until the meat is evenly browned.

Add half the marinade, the reserved chicken, tomatoes, both tomato sauces, jalapenos, and 1 tablespoon of liquid hot pepper sauce to the pot.

Melt the butter in a heavy skillet over medium heat. Add the fresh chiles, mushrooms, and a small amount of the Sauterne and cook for 3 minutes. Add this to the pot. Bring to a boil and simmer, uncovered, for at least 3 hours. When the chili is cooking, from time to time stir in the remaining marinade, the remaining Sauterne and beer. If more liquid is needed, stir in the water in which the chicken was cooked. Taste and adjust seasonings.

Green Garlic Chili

3 pounds fresh pork, cubed in small pieces or
   coarsely ground
1/2 cup olive oil
3 cloves fresh garlic
Salt and white pepper to taste
1 large onion
6 to 8 fresh New Mexico green chiles or
   2 to 4 small cans whole green chiles, chopped
3 large fresh, home grown GREEN tomatoes

Heat oil in heavy Dutch oven or stainless pot. Cook pork until it is white and braised on all sides. Remove pork from pot. Sauté garlic and onion in oil until onion is clear. (Don't chop garlic; sauté peeled, whole cloves.)

Chop tomatoes and green chiles; add them to the onion-garlic mix. Sauté. Put pork back into the pot. Add enough water to cover and simmer, covered, for about 1 1/2 to 2 hours, until pork is done and chili is thick and rich looking. You may need to add more water during the cooking process. Stir to prevent sticking.

This is great alone or served in flour tortillas with plenty of picante sauce.

Green Tomato Chili

2 pounds ground chuck
1 small onion
2 medium green tomatoes
1 envelope chili seasoning
1 teaspoon garlic salt
1 can red kidney beans, drained
1 (16 ounce) can tomato sauce
1 tablespoon green chiles

Brown ground chuck in skillet. Do not drain liquid. Add diced green tomatoes and tomato sauce. Add diced onion and remaining ingredients. Simmer until mixture thickens.

Gringo Chili

Yield: 4 servings

2 teaspoons lard, butter or bacon drippings
1/2 medium onion, coarsely chopped
1 pound beef round, coarse grind
2 tablespoons ground hot red chile
1 tablespoon ground mild red chile
1/4 teaspoon dried Mexican oregano
1/4 teaspoon ground cumin
2 medium garlic cloves, finely chopped
2 cans tomato soup
1 can onion soup
2 (16 ounce) cans kidney beans

Melt the lard, butter or drippings in a large heavy pot over medium heat. Add the onion and cook until it is translucent.

Combine the meat with the ground chile, oregano, cumin, and garlic. Add this meat-and-spice mixture to the pot. Break up and lumps with a fork and cook, stirring occasionally, until the meat is evenly browned.

Stir in the tomato soup, onion soup, and beans. Bring to a boil, then lower the heat and simmer, uncovered, for 1/2 hour until the liquids cook down and the mixture thickens. Taste and adjust seasonings.

Hearty Santa Fe Chili

1 pound lean ground beef or ground chuck
1 onion, chopped
2 (10 ounce) cans diced tomatoes and green chilies (Rotel)
2 cups water
1 (16 ounce) can kidney beans
1 (15 ounce) can pinto beans
1 (15 ounce) can black beans
1 (15 ounce) can fiesta corn
1 (1 ounce) package ranch dressing mix
1 (1.25 ounce) package taco seasoning mix

Sauté beef and onion in a large, heavy saucepan, stirring constantly to keep from sticking; rinse and drain to remove any grease. Stir in tomatoes and green chilies, water, beans, corn and seasoning mixes. Stir and bring to a boil; reduce heat. Simmer for 30-45 minutes, stirring occasionally.

If desired with reduced-fat Cheddar or Monterey jack cheese and sour cream.

Yield: 10-12 servings

Hearty Turkey Chili

1 cup chopped onions
1 cup chopped green bell pepper
2 cloves garlic, minced
1 tablespoon vegetable oil
2 pounds ground raw turkey
2 (14 1/2 ounce) cans tomatoes, cut into
bite-size pieces
1 (12 ounce) bottle chili sauce
1 tablespoon chili powder
1 teaspoon lemon pepper seasoning
1 teaspoon dried basil leaves, crushed
1/2 teaspoon dried thyme leaves, crushed
1/8 to 1/4 teaspoon hot pepper sauce
2 (15 1/2 ounce) cans kidney beans,
drained
Sliced scallions
Shredded Cheddar cheese
Dairy sour cream or plain yogurt

In Dutch oven, sauté onions, green pepper
and garlic in oil. Add turkey and cook until
lightly browned. Add tomatoes, chili sauce,
chili powder, lemon pepper, basil, thyme
and hot pepper sauce. Cover; simmer 45
minutes.

Add kidney beans; simmer an additional 20
minutes.

Serve topped with scallions, cheese and sour cream.

Makes 8 servings (about 9 cups).

Hillbilly Chili

1 pound lean ground beef
Salt and pepper, to taste
4 cans tomatoes, crushed
4 cans pinto beans
1 envelope chili seasoning
Chili powder, to taste
Jalapeño pepper juice, to taste
1 to 2 tablespoons vinegar

Brown ground beef in large saucepan, stirring until crumbly; drain. Season with salt and pepper. Add tomatoes and beans. Cook over medium heat until bubbly. Add chili seasoning, chili powder, and pepper juice. Simmer, covered, for 30 minutes.

Stir in vinegar to bring out the flavor of the spices just before serving.

Hominy Chili with Beans

2 teaspoons vegetable oil
2 teaspoons bottled minced garlic
4 teaspoons chili powder
1 teaspoon ground cumin
1 (15.5 ounce) can white hominy, drained
1 (15.5 z.) can red beans, drained
1 (14.5 ounce) can diced tomatoes, undrained
1 (14.5 ounce) can stewed tomatoes, undrained and chopped
1/4 cup sour cream
1/4 cup (1 ounce) shredded sharp Cheddar cheese
4 teaspoons minced fresh cilantro

Heat oil in a large saucepan over medium heat. Add garlic; sauté 1 minute. Stir in chili powder and next 5 ingredients (chili powder through stewed tomatoes); bring to a boil. Reduce heat; simmer, uncovered, for 15 minutes.

Spoon 1 1/4 cups chili into each bowl (serve 4) top each serving with 1 tablespoon sour cream, 1 tablespoon cheese and 1 teaspoon cilantro.

Hot Chicken Chili

18 chicken wings
Oil (for frying)
1 quart tomatoes
2 or 3 jalapeño peppers, chopped
2 or 3 cups water
Flour
2 (16 ounce) cans kidney beans, drained
Salt and pepper, to taste
1 small onion, chopped

Roll chicken wings in flour and fry in hot oil until crisp. Transfer to serving platter. Remove seeds from jalapeño peppers and chop.

Combine jalapeños, kidney beans and remaining ingredients in skillet where wings were fried (don't throw the grease away). Heat thoroughly, pour over wings and serve.

Serves 4.

Huntsman's Chili

2 tablespoons vegetable oil
1 1/2 pounds venison, cut into 1 1/2-inch cubes
2 medium onions, cut into 1/2-inch pieces
2 medium carrots, peeled and cut into 1/2-inch pieces
2 small parsnips, peeled and cut into 1/2-inch pieces
1/4 cup currants or raisins
4 cloves garlic, minced
3 tablespoons chili powder
2 tablespoons all-purpose flour
1/2 teaspoon salt
1/2 teaspoon ground cumin
1/4 teaspoon ground red pepper
1 (15 ounce) can dark red kidney beans, rinsed and drained
1 (14 1/2 ounce) can diced tomatoes
1 (12 ounce) can beer or 1 1/2 cups beef broth
1 cup water
Fresh cilantro sprigs, snipped

In a 4-quart pot heat oil. Add half of the venison; cook with onion until browned. Add remaining venison, carrots, parsnips, currants or raisins, and garlic. Cook for 5 minutes; stir in chili powder, flour, salt, cumin and red pepper. Add drained beans, undrained tomatoes, beer or broth and water.

Bring to boiling; reduce heat. Simmer, covered, for 1 hour, stirring often.

To serve, ladle into bowls and top with cilantro.

Makes 6 servings.

Louisiana Chili

8 servings

2 pounds lean ground pork
2 large onions, chopped
4 cloves garlic, minced
1 red bell pepper, chopped
1 green bell pepper, chopped
3 stalks celery, chopped
1 (28 ounce) can tomatoes
1 (28 ounce) can kidney beans, drained
and rinsed
1 teaspoon oregano
1/4 teaspoon red pepper flakes
1/4 teaspoon cayenne pepper
Dash hot pepper sauce
Pepper to taste

In a large heavy skillet, cook ground pork over medium heat, breaking up pieces, about 10 minutes or until browned. Drain any fat. Transfer to large saucepan or Dutch oven. Add onions; cook 5 minutes. Add garlic, peppers and celery; cook 5 minutes. Add tomatoes, breaking up with a spoon. Add remaining ingredients. Bring to a boil; reduce heat and simmer, covered, 30 minutes. Add a small amount of water if necessary.

Mescalero Chili

Yield: 8 servings

3 pounds rough ground beef
2 pounds rough ground pork
2 medium onions, chopped
5 cloves garlic, minced
2 tablespoons soy sauce
1 tablespoon Tabasco sauce
2 cups tomato sauce
1/2 cup tomato paste
1/2 cup chopped green bell pepper
1/2 cup chopped red bell pepper
5 whole jalapeno peppers
6 tablespoons Masa Harina
1 (12 ounce) can beer
12 ounces water
3 tablespoons ground cumin
1 teaspoon honey

Put beer and water into a large pot and bring to a boil. Add tomato sauce, soy sauce, and salt to taste. Fry meat and then add to pot.

Sauté the onions and bell peppers in the meat grease and add to pot. Add tomato paste and all other ingredients.

Cook for 45 minutes, stirring often.

Mexican Baked Chili

1 pound lean ground beef
1 can chili beans, drained
1 pint jar salsa
12 ounces Mexican cheese

Brown beef and add beans and salsa. cook over low heat until most of the liquid is gone. Pour into a casserole dish and cover the top with cheese. Bake at 350 degrees F until cheese is melted.

Serve with nachos or Fritos Scoops.

Mouth of Hell

Yield: 6 servings

1 large onion, chopped
2 tablespoons peanut oil
2 pounds rough ground beef brisket
2 cups stewed tomatoes
1 1/2 cups tomato sauce
1 teaspoon molasses
1 tablespoon ground cumin
2 teaspoons paprika
1 cup (12 ounces) beer
3 cloves garlic crushed
5 tablespoons HOT chili powder
1 teaspoon salt
2 tablespoons cayenne flakes
2 tablespoons Masa Harina
1 ounce 150-proof tequila

Sauté the onion and garlic in the oil. Add the meat and sauté meat is browned. Add all remaining ingredients except the tequila and cook for 1 hour 15 minutes.

Pour the tequila over the top of the chili in the bowl when serving.

Nevada Cowboy Chili

1/2 cup lard
3 medium onions, coarsely chopped
2 green bell peppers
2 celery stalks, coarsely chopped
1 tablespoon pickled jalapeno peppers
8 pounds coarse grind beef chuck
30 ounces stewed tomatoes
15 ounces tomato sauce
6 ounces tomato paste
8 tablespoons ground red hot chile
4 tablespoons ground red mild chile
2 teaspoon ground cumin
3 bay leaves
1 tablespoon liquid hot pepper sauce
Garlic salt to taste
Onion salt to taste
Salt to taste
Fresh ground black pepper
4 ounces beer
Water

Heat the lard in a large heavy pot over medium high heat. Add the onions, peppers, celery, and jalapenos. Cook, stirring, until the onions are translucent. Add the meat to the pot. Break up any lumps with a fork and cook, stirring occasionally, until the meat is evenly browned. Stir in the remaining ingredients with enough water to cover. Bring to a boil, then lower the heat and simmer, uncovered, for 3 hours. Stir often. Taste and adjust seasonings.

New Mexico Red Chili

When you order chili in New Mexico, this is what will be served to you.

6 to 8 dried red chiles, stems removed
2 pounds pork, cut into 1 1/2-inch cubes
2 tablespoons vegetable oil
3 cloves garlic, minced
3 cups water or beef broth
Salt, to taste

Place the chiles on a baking sheet in a 250 degree F oven and toast for 15 minutes, being careful not to let them burn. Place the chiles in a saucepan, cover with water, and simmer for 15 minutes until soft. Place them in a blender with the water, and purée until smooth.

Brown the pork in the oil. Add the garlic and sauté. Pour off any excess fat. Combine the chile mixture, pork and remaining water, bring to a boil, then reduce the heat and simmer until the pork is very tender and starts to fall apart — at least 2 hours.

Old Buffalo Breath Chili

1 (5 pound) chuck roast, at least 3 inches
thick
10 to 11 garlic cloves, crushed
Salt, to taste
Chili powder
1/4 cup olive oil
About 1 to 2 cups beef broth
Juice of 1 Mexican lime
2 teaspoons ground dried mild red chile,
such as ancho or New Mexican
2 teaspoons ground dried hot red chile,
such as cayenne or chile de arbol
1 tablespoon cumin seed, toasted and
ground
2 teaspoons Mexican oregano
Chiles pequíns, to taste
Masa Harina, as needed

Two or three hours before you plan to be-
gin making the chili, rub the chuck roast
well with a mash made from two to three of
the garlic cloves and salt. Sprinkle the
meat with the chili powder to lightly coat it.
Loosely cover it with plastic, and set it
aside.

Light enough hardwood charcoal to sear
the meat on an outdoor grill, preferably one
with a cover. At the same time, soak a few
handfuls of mesquite chips in water. When
the coals are covered with gray ash,
spread them out evenly, and scatter the

damp mesquite chips on top. Then immediately set the meat over the smoke, about
an inch from the coals. Cover the grill, and
adjust the dampers to maintain a slow,
steady heat. Let the meat sear for about 12
minutes (this process is meant to flavor,
not cook, the meat), and turn it over to sear
the other side for the same amount of time.
Remove the meat from the heat, saving
any juices on its surface, and transfer it to
the refrigerator. Let it cool thoroughly,
about 1 hour.

When the meat has cooled, trim away any
surface fat or cartilage. With a sharp knife,
cube the meat into the smallest pieces you
have patience for, saving all the juices.

Heat the olive oil in a large, heavy Dutch
oven over moderate heat. Mix in the remaining garlic, and sauté it until it turns
translucent. Stir in the meat and all reserved meat juices, adding just enough
beef broth to cover. Pour in the lime juice,
and sprinkle in the remaining seasonings,
stirring and tasting as you do. Crumble in a
few whole chiles pequíns to bring the heat
up to taste. Turn the heat down as low as
possible. Long cooking toughens, not ten-
derizes, if the chili is allowed to boil. Every
half hour or so, stir the chili and taste for
seasoning, adjusting as you wish. After the
first hour, thicken the chili as you like by
adding the Masa Harina a teaspoon at a
time. The chili should be ready to eat in 3
hours, although it will benefit from a night's
aging in the refrigerator.

Serve the chili steaming hot in large, heavy
bowls with an ample supply of soda crackers and a side of beans, but not much else

except maybe hot black coffee, iced tea or beer.

Old=Fashioned Brick Chili

5 pounds lean chili meat
1 pound suet, ground
4 medium onions, chopped
1 tablespoon salt
1 tablespoon black pepper
1 tablespoon garlic powder
1 1/2 tablespoons cumin powder
1/2 tablespoon red pepper
4 or 5 chile peppers, parboiled, skinned
and finely chopped
3 large tablespoons chili powder

Put suet in pan, let melt, then add onions. Add chili meat and cook until meat stands apart, about 15 to 20 minutes.

Add remaining ingredients except chili powder; turn to low and cook slowly until tender, about 2 1/2 to 3 hours.

About 15 minutes before meat is done, add chili powder and simmer. Pour into rectangular bowls in refrigerator to thicken. This will keep for weeks.

Overnight Dutch Oven Chili

2 pounds ground beef
1/4 cup vegetable oil
1 medium onion, chopped
3 (14 ounce) cans sliced stewed tomatoes
2 (14 ounce) cans clear beef broth
1 (10 ounce) can French onion soup
1 (10 ounce) can tomato soup
20 ounces V-8 juice
2 (1 pound) cans red kidney beans, undrained
4 tablespoons packed light brown sugar
1 tablespoon dark vinegar
2 tablespoons chili powder
1 tablespoon cumin powder
1/8 teaspoon ground anise (optional)
1/2 teaspoon garlic salt

In a 6-quart Dutch oven, brown ground beef in oil until all the pink is gone. Crumble with the back of a fork while it is browning. Remove from heat, and add remaining ingredients.
Cover Dutch oven, and bake at 275 degrees F for 15 hours.

Serves 8 to 10, and leftovers freeze well.

Pennsylvania Dutch Oven Chili

1 pound homemade noodles or 1 (12 to 16 ounce)
   bag wide egg noodles
1 can baked beans
1 cup spaghetti sauce or less (or 1 small jar)
1 pound hamburger
1 onion, chopped

Brown hamburger and onion. Cook and drain egg noodles. Combine everything. You may need additional sauce if you have leftovers and warm them up later. Chili should be thick, not soupy.

Serve with crusty bread.

Prize-Winning Chili

3/4 cup Masa Harina
1/2 to 1 tablespoon salt, depending on taste
1/2 teaspoon black pepper
3 pounds beef, cut into 1/2 inch cubes
3 tablespoons vegetable oil
3 medium onions, chopped
6 large cloves garlic, minced
2 Serrano or jalapeño chiles, minced
1 dried chipotle chile pod
3 ancho chile pods
1 dried New Mexico chile pod
4 New Mexico chiles, roasted, peeled and seeded
6 cups beef broth
1 tablespoon ground cumin

Remove stems, seeds, and veins from dried chiles. Place both dried and roasted chiles and 1 1/2 cups of broth in a saucepan. Boil 5 minutes, then steep 15 minutes.

Combine Masa Harina, salt and pepper in a paper bag. Add meat to bag and shake to coat.

Place oil in a Dutch oven or heavy pot. Heat at high temperature until oil almost just starts to smoke. Add meat, stirring constantly to prevent sticking. Add onions, garlic and jalapeños or serranos. Cook and stir until soft.

Add 4 1/2 cups of beef broth and bring to a boil. Reduce heat and simmer. Purée all the peppers and liquid in a food processor or blender. Add purée to meat and stir. Cover and simmer 2 to 3 hours, or until meat is tender.

Add cumin. Add salt to taste. If needed, thicken with additional Masa Harina and a little water.

Pumpkin Chili

1 medium pumpkin, 4 to 5 pound, or 2 cup solid pack pumpkin
1 small yellow onion, chopped
1 clove garlic, minced
1 red bell pepper, cored, diced
2 tablespoons vegetable oil
1 pound lean ground turkey or beef
4 cups diced tomatoes
2 cups tomato sauce
2 cups cooked kidney beans
1 cup whole corn kernels
1/2 cup diced green chilies, to taste
1 tablespoon chili powder
1 teaspoon ground cumin
Salt and fresh black pepper

Cut lid in top of pumpkin; set aside. Remove seeds and pith; replace lid. Bake at 375 degrees F for 20 minutes. Scoop out pumpkin flesh, leaving at least 1/2-inch to hold pumpkin shape. Dice pumpkin and set aside. Reserve pumpkin shell.

In 6-quart saucepan, sauté onion, garlic and bell pepper in oil 5 minutes or until tender. Add ground meat; cook, stirring, until browned. Drain. Add tomatoes, tomato sauce, reserved pumpkin (2 to 3 cups fresh or 2 cups canned), kidney beans, corn, chilies, chili powder, cumin, salt and pepper. Bring to a boil; reduce heat, cover,

simmer 30 minutes or to desired consistency. Stir often.

Adjust seasoning. Serve from reserved
pumpkin shell. Garnish if desired with
shredded cheese and sour cream. Serve
over cooked rice.

Makes six to eight servings.

Pumpkin Chili Mexicana

2 tablespoons vegetable oil
1/2 cup chopped onion
1 cup chopped red or green bell pepper
1 clove garlic, finely chopped
1 pound ground turkey
2 (14 ounce) cans diced tomatoes, undrained
1 3/4 cups pumpkin purée
1 (15 ounce) can tomato sauce
1 (15 1/4 ounce) can kidney beans, drained
1 (4 ounce) can diced green chiles
1/2 cup whole kernel corn
1 tablespoon chili powder
1 teaspoon ground cumin
1 teaspoon salt
1/2 teaspoon ground black pepper

Heat vegetable oil in large saucepan over medium-high heat. Add onion, bell pepper and garlic; cook, stirring 5 to 7 minutes or until tender. Add turkey; cook until browned. Drain.

Add tomatoes with juice, pumpkin, tomato sauce, beans chiles, corn, chili powder, cumin, salt and pepper. Reduce heat to low. Cover; cook, stirring occasionally for 30 minutes.

Rattlesnake Chili

3/4 cup chopped onion
3 tablespoons oil
2 1/2 cups parboiled rattlesnake meat
2 cups cooked tomatoes
2 cups cooked pinto beans
2 1/2 teaspoons chili powder
1/2 teaspoon hot red pepper flakes
1 teaspoon salt

In a large skillet, sauté onion in hot oil until tender. Add remaining ingredients. Simmer for 15 to 20 minutes. Serve as is or over rice.

Makes 4 to 5 servings.

Red Chile Paste

This is the basis for enchiladas and chile con carne.

24 dried red chiles
2 tablespoons mashed garlic
1 teaspoon salt
2 quarts water or to cover

Wash whole dry chile pods. Wearing rubber gloves, remove stems, veins and seeds. Cover chiles with water in a heavy kettle, then bring to a boil. Lower heat and cook slowly for 30 minutes. Drain. Put through a colander or sieve after testing to make sure the pulp separates easily from the skin. Add garlic and salt to the pulp. Blend smooth for a pure, thick chile paste.

Red Chili Nightmare

Yield: 4 servings

1 cup dried pinto beans
5 cups water
2 tablespoons lard
1 tablespoon bacon drippings
1 onion
12 ounces country-style pork sausage
1 pound beef, coarse grind
4 garlic cloves
1 teaspoon anise
1/2 teaspoon coriander seeds
1/2 teaspoon fennel seeds
1/2 teaspoon ground cloves
1 (1-inch) cinnamon stick, ground
1 teaspoon freshly ground black pepper
1 teaspoon paprika
1 whole nutmeg, ground
1 teaspoon cumin
2 teaspoons dried Mexican oregano
4 tablespoons sesame seeds
1 cup blanched almonds, skins removed
12 whole dried red chiles or 1 1/2 cup chile
Caribe
1 1/2 ounces milk chocolate, small pieces
1 (6 ounce) can tomato paste
2 tablespoons vinegar
3 teaspoons lemon juice
1 soft tortilla, chopped
Salt

Place the rinsed beans in a bowl, add 2 to 3 cups of water and soak overnight. Check the beans occasionally and add water as necessary to keep them moist.

Pour the beans and the water in which they were soaked into a heavy saucepan and add 2 to 3 more cups of water. Bring to a boil over medium-high heat, then lower heat and simmer, partially covered, for about 45 minutes, until the beans are cooked but still firm. Check occasionally and add water if necessary. Drain the beans, reserving the cooking liquid.

Melt the lard in a heavy skillet over medium heat. Add the beans and lightly fry them in the lard. Set aside.

Melt the drippings in a large heavy pot over medium heat. Add the onion and cook until it is translucent.

Combine the sausage and the beef with all the spices up through the oregano. Add this meat and spice mixture to the pot with the onion. Break up any lumps with a fork and cook, stirring occasionally, until the meat is very well browned.

Add the reserved bean-cooking liquid to the pot. Stir in all the remaining ingredients. Bring to a boil, then lower the heat and cook, uncovered, for 1/2 hour longer. Stir occasionally. Add water only if necessary to maintain the consistency of a chunky soup.

Taste when curiosity becomes unbearable and courage is strong. Adjust seasonings.

Reno Red Chili

Yield: 6 servings

1 (3 pound) round steak, coarsely ground
1 (3 pound) chuck steak, coarsely ground
1 cup vegetable oil or suet
Black pepper to taste
3 ounces Gebhardt Chili Powder
6 tablespoons cumin
2 tablespoons MSG
6 small cloves garlic, minced
2 medium onions, chopped
6 dried chile pods, seeded and stemmed, boiled
    30 minutes in water OR 1 (3 ounce) bottle New Mexico pepper
1 tablespoon oregano, brewed in 1/2 cup Budweiser beer (like tea)
2 tablespoons paprika
2 tablespoons cider vinegar
3 cups beef broth
1 (4 ounce) can diced green chiles
1 (14 ounce) can stewed tomatoes
1 teaspoon Tabasco sauce, or to taste
2 tablespoons Masa Harina

Brown meat in oil or fat, adding black pepper to taste. Drain meat and add chili powder, cumin, MSG, garlic and chopped onion. Cook for 30 to 45 minutes using as little liquid as possible. Add water only as necessary. Stir often.

Remove skins from boiled chile pods. Mash the pulp and add to meat mixture. Strain oregano tea, then add to meat mixture along with paprika, vinegar, 2/3 of the beef broth, green chiles, stewed tomatoes and Tabasco sauce. Simmer for 30 to 45 minutes, stirring often.

Dissolve Masa Harina in remaining beef broth then pour into chili. Simmer another 30 minutes, stirring often.

Saddlebag Chili

Yield: 8 servings

4 pounds beef brisket (rough ground)
3 medium onions, coarsely chopped
5 cloves garlic, minced
6 slices bacon
1 (12 ounce) can beer
2 ounces sour mash whiskey
2 tablespoons blackstrap molasses
1/2 teaspoon allspice
1 teaspoon salt, or to taste
4 tablespoons ground cumin
1/2 cup tomato paste
3 cups tomato sauce
1 teaspoon Worcestershire sauce
1 green bell pepper, chopped
1 red bell pepper, chopped
2 tablespoons cayenne pepper flakes
8 fresh whole jalapeno peppers
2 tablespoons Tabasco sauce
1/4 cup Masa Harina

Fry bacon, reserving the grease. Save bacon for another use. Sauté the onions and bell peppers in the bacon grease with 1/2 of the minced garlic. Fry brisket.

Pour the beer and the whiskey into a large pot and turn heat to medium high. Add sautéed onions and peppers, tomato sauce, jalapenos and 3/4 of the cumin, the Worcestershire sauce, cayenne flakes and

Tabasco sauce. When mixture begins to boil, reduce heat to medium and add remaining ingredients except the 1 remaining tablespoon cumin. Cook on medium-low to low heat for 1 hour, stirring frequently.

Add the remaining cumin and cook for another 10 to 15 minutes over medium-high heat, stirring constantly.

Seafood Chili

1 tablespoon vegetable oil
2 celery stalks
1 leek, chopped
2 cloves garlic, minced
1 teaspoon ground cumin
1 (28 ounce) can diced tomatoes
1 1/2 teaspoons Tabasco sauce
1/2 teaspoon salt
8 ounces bay scallops or small shrimp
6 ounces lump crabmeat, picked over to
remove any cartilage
Chopped cilantro
2 cups hot cooked rice

Heat oil in a 4-quart saucepan over medium heat. Add celery, leek and garlic.
Cook until tender, stirring occasionally, 5
minutes. Add cumin; cook 1 minute.

Stir in tomatoes with their liquid, hot pepper
sauce and salt. Heat to boiling over high
heat. Reduce heat to low; cover. Simmer
15 minutes to blend flavors.

Stir in scallops and crabmeat; heat to boiling. Cook 3 minutes or until seafood is tender.

Serve over rice. Sprinkle chili with chopped cilantro.

Makes 6 servings.

Southern Chili

1 1/2 pounds ground meat
1 large onion, chopped
2 cloves garlic, finely chopped
2 1/2 teaspoons salt
3/4 teaspoon pepper
1 teaspoon chili powder
2 cans tomato paste
2 tomato paste cans water
1 (No. 2) can tomato juice
2 tablespoons granulated sugar
2 cans chili beans, drained

Brown meat with onion, garlic, 1 1/2 teaspoons of the salt, 1/2 teaspoon of the pepper and chili powder.

Combine remaining salt and pepper with remaining ingredients except beans; add to meat mixture. Bring to a boil; simmer for 2 hours. Add beans during final 15 minutes of cooking.

Yields 6 to 8 servings.

Southwestern White Chili

1 tablespoon olive oil
1/2 pound boneless, skinless chicken
breast, cut into small cubes
1/4 cup chopped onion
1 cup chicken broth
1 (4 ounce) can chopped green chiles
1 (19 ounce) can white kidney beans (can-
nelloni), undrained
2 green onions, sliced
1 teaspoon garlic powder
1 teaspoon ground cumin
1/2 teaspoon oregano
1/2 teaspoon cilantro (optional)
1/8 teaspoon ground red pepper
Monterey jack cheese (optional)

Heat oil in large skillet over medium-high
heat. Add chicken and onions; cook 4 to 5
minutes.

Stir in broth, chiles and spices. Simmer 15
minutes.

Stir in beans; simmer 5 minutes. Top with
green onions and Monterey jack cheese, if
you desire.

Speakeasy Chili

5 pounds ground round
Salt and pepper
1 tablespoon chili powder (more if desired)
1 (16 ounce) can dark red kidney beans
1 (16 ounce) can light red kidney beans
2 (16 ounce) cans small red beans
1 tablespoon vegetable oil
3 large green bell peppers, cored and chopped
3 jalapeno peppers, cored and chopped
1 large red onion, chopped
1 large Spanish onion, chopped
1 large white or yellow onion, chopped
8 to 10 cloves garlic, finely chopped
4 (28 ounce) cans diced tomatoes
3 (64 ounce) cans tomato juice
Chili powder to taste
Salt and pepper

Break up and cook meat in large frying pan until browned and crumbly. Drain thoroughly. Season with salt, pepper, and at least 1 tablespoon of chili powder. Set aside.

Sauté green peppers, jalapenos, onions and garlic in oil until limp. Add tomatoes and juice from pan into a large pot. Add hamburger, sautéed vegetables, and beans to pot. Add tomato juice until chili is soupy, not too thick. Season with chili powder to taste. Simmer for 90 minutes, stirring frequently to prevent scorching.

Leftover chili can be frozen.

Spicy Pineapple Pork Chili

1 pound lean boneless pork, trimmed of fat and
   cut into 1-inch cubes
1 cup dried small white beans, rinsed, drained
   and picked over
1 cup hot water
1 (14 1/2 ounce) can diced tomatoes in purée
1 (6 ounce) can tomato paste
1 (20 ounce) can unsweetened pineapple chunks,
   drained, juice reserved
1 (4 ounce) can diced green chiles
1 medium onion, chopped
1 tablespoon chili powder
1 tablespoon ground cumin
1/2 teaspoon garlic powder

In a 3 1/2-quart electric crockpot, combine the pork, beans, hot water, tomatoes with their liquid, tomato paste, juice drained from the pineapple chunks, chiles, onion, chili powder, cumin and garlic powder. Mix well.

Cover and cook on the LOW heat setting 8 1/2 to 9 hours, until the pork and beans are tender, stirring once halfway through the cooking time, if possible. Stir in the pineapple chunks and serve.

Makes 4 to 6 servings.

Texas Chili

Olive oil
1 (3 pound) chuck roast, cut into 1-inch cubes
3 onions, minced
5 cloves garlic, minced
1/4 cup chili powder
1 teaspoon oregano
2 teaspoons cumin
2 tablespoons Masa Harina
1 jalapeño pepper, minced
Cheddar cheese, shredded

When preparing the meat, remove as much fat as possible.

Heat olive oil to smoking in a heavy kettle and add meat. Cook until meat is light colored. Add onions and garlic. Add 2 to 3 cups water to cover and mix. Bring to a boil, then cover and simmer for 1 hour.

Add chili powder, oregano, cumin and salt; cook slowly for 1 hour more, stirring occasionally.

Stir Masa Harina into 1/4 cup of cold water. Add to chili. Add jalapeño peppers. Continue to cook until the chili thickens, about

10 to 15 minutes, stirring frequently to avoid sticking.

NOTE: Masa Harina, a finely ground white cornmeal, is available in the Mexican section of many supermarkets, but coarse cornmeal, ground in a blender or food processor for several minutes can be substituted.

Per serving: 996 Calories; 57g Fat (51% calories from fat); 62g Protein; 60g Carbohydrate; 197mg Cholesterol; 256mg Sodium

Texas Chili II

1 (3 pound) round steak, cut into 3/4-inch cubes
1 pound ground chuck
1 pound pinto beans
2 quarts tomatoes
1 pound yellow onions
3 sweet bell peppers
5 dried chile peppers
1/2 cup chili powder
Salt
Red pepper
1/4 cup Crisco
2 tablespoons Crisco
1/2 gallon water
1/4 cup granulated sugar

Soak pinto beans in 1/2 gallon water overnight in refrigerator.

In a 10- to 12-inch skillet, brown round steak in the 1/4 cup Crisco, stirring frequently.

In another skillet, brown ground chuck on low heat, stirring frequently for 10 minutes.

Cut up onions and bell peppers in 1/2-inch pieces. Add to ground chuck with 2 tablespoons Crisco and sauté for approximately 15 minutes, stirring frequently.

Mince chile peppers very fine.

In a large 8-quart or larger kettle, combine pinto beans, browned round steak, sautéed ground chuck, onions, peppers, 2 quarts tomatoes, minced chile peppers and the 1/2 cup chili powder; cook covered on simmer for 2 hours.

Add salt and red pepper to taste. Add sugar and simmer for 4 hours. Add additional water sparingly, if necessary.

Taste and add more chili powder, salt, red pepper and sugar as desired. Simmer 1 hour (total cooking time is 7 hours).

Serve with Texas toast or oyster crackers and ice cold milk or iced tea.

Texas Red Chili

2 tablespoons vegetable oil
2 large onions, coarsely chopped
5 cloves garlic, crushed
2 to 2 1/2 pounds lean boneless beef, cut into 1/2-inch cubes
3 tablespoons Gebhardt chili powder
1 tablespoon paprika
1 teaspoon crushed dried hot peppers
2 teaspoons cumin
2 teaspoons Mexican oregano
1 cup hot water
1 teaspoon salt
1 to 2 tablespoons Masa Harina

In a large Dutch oven heat the oil over medium heat. Add the onions and garlic and sauté until very lightly browned. Add the beef cubes in several batches and brown on all sides. When all the beef is browned, add all remaining ingredients except the Masa Harina. Bring to a simmer, then cover and cook over low heat for 3 to 4 hours until the meat is very tender. If too much of the liquid cooks away, add some more hot water during the cooking. Adjust salt and chili powder, adding more to taste if desired.

To thicken the chili, mix the Masa Harina with a little cold water, then add this to the chili while it is still simmering. Cook the chili 10 to 15 minutes longer.

Serve the chili in bowls with saltines and cooked pinto beans on the side.

Turkey Chili

1/4 cup olive oil
3 pounds raw ground turkey
Water
6 tablespoons chili powder
3 teaspoons salt, or to taste
10 cloves garlic, peeled and minced
1 1/2 teaspoons ground cumin
1 teaspoon ground marjoram
1 teaspoon ground red pepper
1/2 teaspoon ground black pepper
1 tablespoon granulated sugar
1 tablespoon unsweetened cocoa powder
3 tablespoons ground paprika
4 tablespoons all-purpose flour
7 tablespoons cornmeal
Cooked pinto or kidney beans (optional)

Heat olive oil in a 6-quart pot. Add ground turkey; sear over high heat. Stir until meat is gray, not brown. Add 1 quart water. Bring to a boil and simmer for 1 hour; skim off fat. Add chili powder, salt, garlic, cumin, marjoram, red pepper, black pepper, sugar, cocoa powder and paprika. Simmer 30 minutes.

In a small bowl, combine flour, cornmeal and 3/4 cup cold water. Stir into turkey mixture; stir for 5 minutes. Mixture will be very thick. Let cool and store in refrigerator.

To serve, add water to make chili of desired consistency. Reheat to simmering; serve hot. Cooked pinto or kidney beans can be added to chili, if desired.

Vegetarian Chili

This spicy chili will warm you on a chilly (no pun intended) evening, and is also very healthful. You can eat it as a thick soup or serve it over cooked spaghetti, as a sort of sauce.

1 onion, minced
1 tablespoon olive oil
1 (16 ounce) can diced tomatoes, undrained
1 cup water
1 sweet bell pepper, diced
1 tablespoon chili powder (or more, to taste)
2/3 cup uncooked barley
1 (15 ounce) can pinto beans, drained
Shredded Cheddar cheese

In a large skillet, sauté onion in olive oil. Add remaining ingredients except beans and cheese. Cover and simmer 35 minutes. Add beans and heat through. Garnish with cheese, if desired.

Venison Bowl of Red

4 tablespoons olive oil
1 large onion, diced
1 pound sweet Italian sausage, removed
from casing
2 teaspoons chili powder
2 teaspoons ground cumin
1 teaspoon dried oregano
1/2 teaspoon red pepper flakes
2 pounds boneless venison shoulder, cut
into 1 1/2-inch cubes
2 cups beef broth
2 cups crushed Italian plum tomatoes, in
juices
1/4 cup tomato paste
1 to 2 tablespoons chipotle chiles in adobo
sauce, to taste
1 tablespoon dark brown sugar
1 red bell pepper, diced
Salt and pepper, to taste
1/4 cup chopped parsley

Place 2 tablespoons of the oil in a large
pot. Add onion; cook over low heat for 10
minutes, stirring. Crumble the sausage
meat into the pot, raise the heat to medium
high and brown well for 10 minutes, stirring
to break up the clumps. As the meat cooks,
sprinkle with the chili powder, cumin, oregano and pepper flakes.

Heat remaining oil in a nonstick skillet.
Brown the venison quickly in small batches

over medium-high heat; add to the pot. Add beef broth, tomatoes (with juices), tomato paste, chipotles and brown sugar. Simmer, uncovered, over medium heat for 1 hour, stirring occasionally. Add bell pepper and simmer 30 minutes more or until venison is tender; do not boil. Season with salt and pepper and stir in the parsley.

Serve in bowls over rice.

White Chicken Chili

1 large onion, chopped (about 1 cup)
1 clove garlic, finely chopped
1/4 cup butter or margarine
4 cups chicken breast, 1/2-inch cubes
3 cups chicken broth
2 tablespoons snipped cilantro or parsley
1 tablespoon dried basil leaves
2 teaspoons ground red chiles
1/4 teaspoon ground cloves
2 (16 ounce) cans great northern beans
1 can white shoe peg corn, drained

Sauté onion and garlic in butter over low heat, stirring until lightly browned. Stir in remaining ingredients. Heat to a boil. Reduce heat and simmer 1 hour, stirring occasionally.

Serve topped with fresh chopped tomatoes, sour cream and tortilla chips.

Makes 6 servings (1 1/2 cups each).

White Lightening Chili

1 pound dried navy beans
4 (14 1/2 ounce) cans chicken broth, divided
1 large onion, chopped
2 cloves garlic, minced
1 tablespoon ground white pepper
1 tablespoon Mexican oregano
1 tablespoon ground cumin
1 teaspoon salt
1/2 teaspoon ground cloves
5 cups chopped cooked chicken
2 (4 ounce) cans chopped green chiles
1 cup water
1 jalapeño pepper, seeded and chopped
8 (8-inch) flour tortillas
Shredded Monterey Jack cheese
Salsa
Sour cream

Sort and wash beans; place in a large Dutch oven. Cover with water 2 inches above beans. Soak 8 hours.

Drain beans and return them to Dutch oven. Discard liquid. Add 3 cans chicken broth and next 7 ingredients; bring mixture to a boil. Reduce heat and simmer, covered, 2 hours or until beans are tender, stirring occasionally. Add remaining can of chicken broth, chicken and next 3 ingredients. Cover and simmer 1 hour, stirring occasionally.

With kitchen shears, make 4 cuts in each tortilla toward, but not through, center. Line serving bowls with tortillas, overlapping cut edges of tortillas. Spoon in chili, and top with cheese, salsa and sour cream. Serve immediately.

Yields 12 cups.

Lightning Source UK Ltd.
Milton Keynes UK
UKOW042225260912

199652UK00001BA/30/A